MARVEL
GUARDIANS OF THE GALAXY
GALAXY'S MOST WANTED

W9-BHX-474

"SO VERY YOUNG" / "SHOW AND TELL"
WRITER: **MAIRGHREAD SCOTT**

"GESUNDHEIT, HANG ON TIGHT!"
WRITER: **PAUL ALLOR**

"ALL HAIL KING GROOT"
WRITER: **JOE CARAMAGNA**

ARTIST: **ADAM ARCHER**
COLORIST: **CHARLIE KIRCHOFF**
LETTERER: **VC'S JOE CARAMAGNA**

"STAR-LORD" / "GAMORA" / "DRAX" / "GROOT & ROCKET"
BASED ON THE TV SERIES WRITTEN BY **MARTY ISENBERG & HENRY GILROY**
DIRECTED BY **LEO RILEY**
ADAPTED BY **JOE CARAMAGNA**

"GALAXY'S MOST WANTED"
WRITER: **WILL CORONA PILGRIM**
ARTIST: **ANDREA DI VITO**
COLORIST: **LAURA VILLARI**
LETTERER: **VC'S CLAYTON COWLES**

COVER ART: **ADAM ARCHER** (#2-3), **JEFF WAMESTER** (#4)
& **JEE-HYUNG LEE** ("GALAXY'S MOST WANTED")
ASSISTANT EDITOR: **MARK BASSO**
EDITORS: **SEBASTIAN GIRNER, JON MOISAN & BILL ROSEMANN**
SENIOR EDITOR: **MARK PANICCIA**

SPECIAL THANKS TO HENRY ONG & PRODUCT FACTORY

COLLECTION EDITOR: **ALEX STARBUCK**
ASSISTANT EDITOR: **SARAH BRUNSTAD**
EDITORS, SPECIAL PROJECTS: **JENNIFER GRÜNWALD & MARK D. BEAZLEY**
SENIOR EDITOR, SPECIAL PROJECTS: **JEFF YOUNGQUIST**
SVP PRINT, SALES & MARKETING: **DAVID GABRIEL**

EDITOR IN CHIEF: **AXEL ALONSO**   CHIEF CREATIVE OFFICER: **JOE QUESADA**
PUBLISHER: **DAN BUCKLEY**   EXECUTIVE PRODUCER: **ALAN FINE**

MARVEL STUDIOS
VP PRODUCTION & DEVELOPMENT: **JONATHAN SCHWARTZ**
SVP PRODUCTION & DEVELOPMENT: **JEREMY LATCHAM**
PRESIDENT: **KEVIN FEIGE**

THE END

3

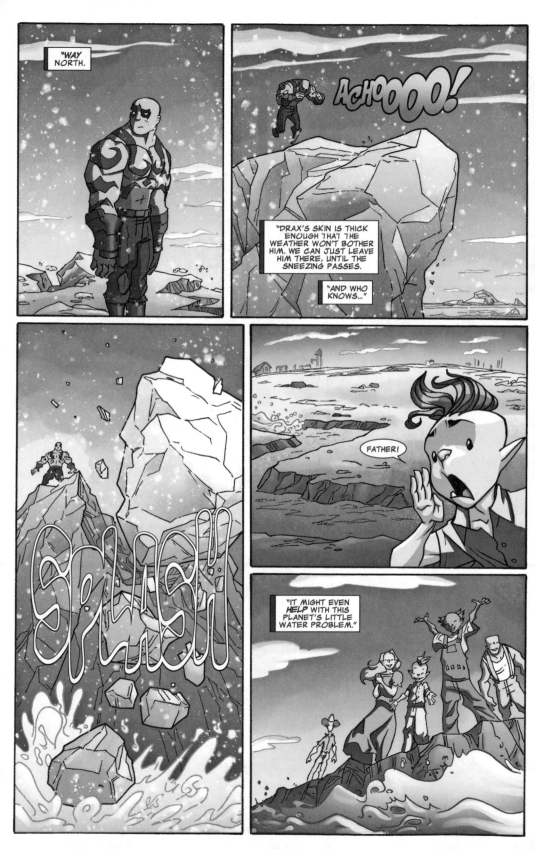

THE END!

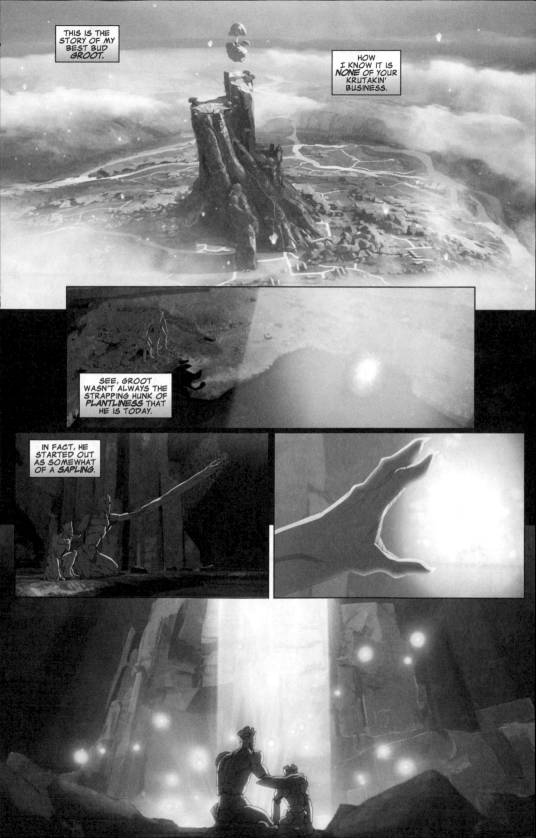

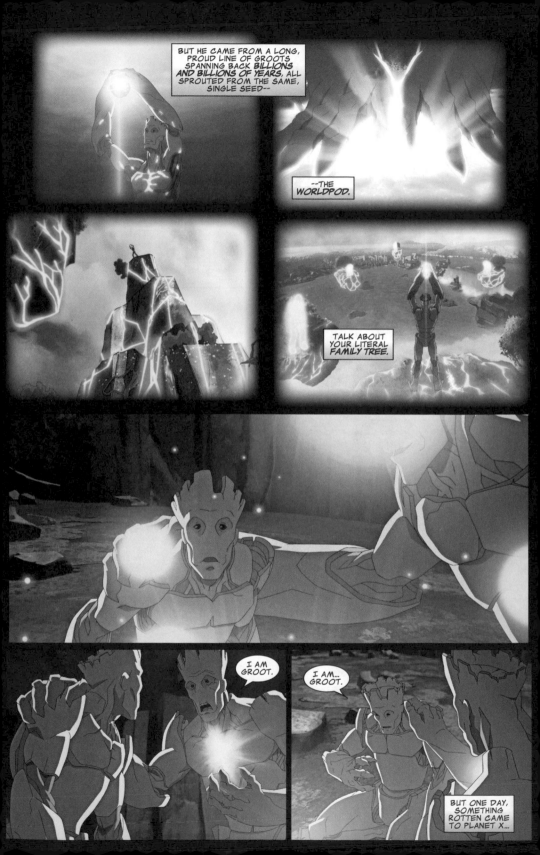

GALAXY'S MOST WANTED

HMMM...

CLICK-CLICK

CH-CHAN

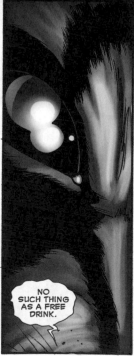

NO SUCH THING AS A FREE DRINK.

NOW WE'RE TALKIN'!

FZZT

C'MON!

HA!

THE END!

When DR. DONALD BLAKE strikes his wooden walking-stick upon the ground, it becomes the mystic hammer MJOLNIR— and the lame physician is transformed into the Norse God of Thunder, Master of the Storm, Lord of the Living Lightning— and heir to the throne of eternal Asgard....

Stan Lee PRESENTS: THE MIGHTY THOR!®

MOON DRAGON--MISTRESS OF MENTAL AND MARTIAL ARTS, TRAINED AND GROOMED BY MENTOR AND SENSIA ON SATURN'S HOLLOW MOON TITAN TO ASSUME THE MANTLE OF CELESTIAL MADONNA...UNTIL ANOTHER WAS CHOSEN IN HER PLACE.

DRAX THE DESTROYER-- ONCE A NORMAL MAN WHO MET HIS DEATH IN A FIERY CAR CRASH AND WHOSE SOUL WAS SHAPED BY THE TITANS MENTOR AND KRONOS INTO A NEW KIND OF BEING WHOSE SOLE REASON FOR EXISTENCE WAS THE DESTRUCTION OF THE DEATH-GOD THANOS.

AND THOR--IMMORTAL LORD OF THUNDER, SON OF ODIN, SCION OF ASGARD, WHO HAS CHOSEN TO CAST HIS LOT AMONG THE MORTAL HUMANS OF EARTH.

NOW, THE FATES OF THESE THREE EXTRAORDINARY BEINGS ARE DESTINED TO INTERTWINE IN--

ACTS OF DESTRUCTION

DOUG MOENCH and KEITH POLLARD / D. GREEN & | JANICE | GEORGE | JIM | JIM
WRITER   LAYOUT ARTIST   P. MARCOS CHIANG ROUSSOS SALICRUP SHOOTER
                              EMBELISHERS LETTERS COLORS EDITOR EDITOR-IN-CHIEF

MEANWHILE, IN THE COLDLY GLITTERING VASTNESS OF NEAR-SPACE, A *STRANGE CRAFT* WANDERS AIMLESSLY.

ITS PILOT AND SOLE PASSENGER IS THE MYSTERIOUS WOMAN KNOWN AS *MOON DRAGON*...

ASIDE FROM MY OCCASIONAL DEALINGS WITH THE AVENGERS, THERE IS NO REASON FOR ME TO REMAIN ON EARTH-- NOTHING TO HOLD ME...

EVEN THOUGH I WAS BORN ON THE PLANET, IT IS NOW DIFFICULT FOR ME TO EMPATHIZE WITH NORMAL HUMANS AND THEIR SMALL AFFAIRS.

AND EVEN TITAN, WHERE I WAS RAISED, NO LONGER HOLDS GREAT ATTRACTION FOR ME, NOT SINCE THE CHOICE WAS MADE.

MENTOR, I ADMIT, WAS AN *EXCELLENT* SURROGATE FATHER--

"-- AS HE AND SENSIA TRAINED ME IN THE MENTAL AND PHYSICAL ARTS, GROOMING ME TO OPPOSE THANOS AND THEN BECOME THE CELESTIAL MADONNA--

"-- SHE WHO IS DESTINED TO BRING NEW COSMIC LIFE TO THE UNIVERSE.

"BUT THEN IMMORTUS CHOSE *MANTIS* TO BECOME THE MADONNA... AND THOUGH I FEEL NO RESENTMENT OR SPITE, THERE *WAS* DISAPPOINTMENT...

"... A CRUEL LACK OF FULFILLMENT..."

... AND NOW I HAVE BEGUN TO FEEL THE FULL VOID OF PURPOSE, DESTINY, COMMITMENT-- AND MY THOUGHTS INCREASINGLY DWELL ON THE PAST... AND ON MY *REAL* FATHER.

MEANWHILE, AT BLAKE'S NEW YORK APARTMENT, THE PHONE RINGS AGAIN.

THIS TIME IT'S MILLIONAIRE INDUSTRIALIST TONY STARK...

HOW ABOUT DINNER NEXT THURSDAY AT EIGHT, DON? I HAVE A PROPOSITION FOR YOU.

SOUNDS GREAT, TONY-- SEE YOU THEN.

THE GLUMNESS RETURNS AS SOON AS HE RACKS THE PHONE...

I FEEL LIKE A MAN WHOSE FUTURE CONSISTS OF TWO EVENTS. I'VE GOT TO DO *SOMETHING*--AND IF BLAKE IS PRETTY MUCH USELESS FOR THE TIME BEING...

...THEN MAYBE IT'S TIME TO *CHANGE* MATTERS, AND BECOME...

BOOM

--THOR THE MIGHTY!

GONE IS THE SIMPLE WALKING STICK, REPLACED BY THE ENCHANTED MALLET MJOLNIR --AND IN THE LAME PHYSICIAN'S PLACE THERE NOW STANDS A GRIM GOD OF THUNDER...

...SCION OF VAUNTED ASGARD, BUT ADOPTED SON OF LOWLY EARTH.

HE SCOURS THE MANHATTAN SKIES, CRAVING SOME SENSE OF PURPOSE, SOME CONSTRUCTIVE COURSE OF ACTION, BUT--

'TIS A RARE, CALM NIGHT-- WHEN EVEN EVIL AND VIOLENCE SEEM CONTENT TO SLUMBER IN PEACE...

AND FOR THAT I SHOULD BE THANKFUL, AS SHOULD ALL THOSE WHO DWELL IN THE CITY-- YET IT DEPRIVES EVEN THOR OF ANY MISSION OR DUTY.

ON PURE WHIM, HE SWERVES SHARPLY TO THE EAST...

IT HAS BEEN SOME TIME SINCE I LAST SAW MY FELLOW AVENGERS. I SHALL TAKE THE PHONE CALL FROM IRON MAN-- IN THE GUISE OF TONY STARK --AS AN OMEN, AND USE THIS IDLE TIME TO VISIT THE MANSION...

MARK GRUENWALD & RALPH MACCHIO
SCRIPTERS

KEITH POLLARD & GENE DAY
ARTISTS

JOE ROSEN
LETTERER

GEORGE ROUSSOS
COLORIST

JIM SALICRUP
EDITOR

JIM SHOOTER
EDITOR-IN-CHIEF

JUDGEMENT -- and LAMENT!

ONCE, GOLDEN RAYS OF SUNLIGHT WARMED *VALHALLA*--THE NORSE DOMAIN OF THE DEAD, WHERE THOSE BRAVE WARRIORS LOST IN COMBAT SPENT A JOYFUL ETERNITY AMID THE SOUND OF ENDLESS BATTLE.

BUT THEN CAME *HELA*, DREAD GODDESS OF *DEATH*, WHO USURPED THIS PLACE WITH HER ICY TOUCH-- REMAKING IT IN THE IMAGE OF HER OWN KINGDOM, *NIFFLE-HEIM*...COLD, CRUEL, FOREBODING.

NOW, *ODIN*, RULER OF THE GODS, HAS COME TO SET THINGS A'RIGHT.

'TWAS NOT ENOW THAT THOU DID FORCIBLY TAKE VALHALLA, HELA. NOW, THOU HAST E'EN SLAIN MY NINE *VALKYRIES*, WHO I DID SEND BEFORE ME.

THOU HAST AT *LAST* GONE TOO FAR-- AND WILL PAY FOR THY MISDEEDS.

I THINK NOT, BRASH ONE, FOR I RULE HERE AND THERE IS NAUGHT THOU CANST DO 'GAINST ME.

LET THE STRENGTH DRAIN FROM THY BODY 'TIL THOU ART HELPLESS. AND LET IT THUS BE KNOWN FORE'ER THAT ODIN BE *SUPREME* O'ER ALL HE DOTH SURVEY.

BUT THAT DOTH MEAN LITTLE TO ME NOW.

THOUGH I HAVE BEEN CALLED OMNISCIENT--STILL DOTH THY MOTIVES BAFFLE ME.

WHY, HELA? WHY HAST THOU DONE THESE THINGS? SPEAK.

MONTHS AGO, WHEN THY SON *THOR* WERT NEAR DEATH, I DID COME TO CLAIM HIM.* BUT THOU DID SEND HIS TRUE BELOVED--*SIF,* TO HIS SIDE, AND SHE DID PLEAD THAT I TAKE HER LIFE IN EXCHANGE FOR THOR'S. SO GREAT WAS HER PASSION--I WAS MOVED AS NE'ER IN MY EXISTENCE.

FEELINGS WERT AWAKENED WITHIN ME...FEELINGS OF COMPASSION--DESIRE... AND LOVE, AT LONG LAST, HELA KNEW WHAT IT MEANT TO BE A WOMAN. BUT, I BE GODDESS OF DEATH AS WELL, AND CAN NE'ER CONSUMMATE THESE LONGINGS...FOR ALL THAT I TOUCH TURNS TO DUST, A TRAGEDY NE'ER TO BE RESOLVED.

* *THOR 190* ** *THOR 278--J.S.*

THEN, OF LATE THOU DID *SET* IN MOTION THE FORCES OF *RAGNAROK* WHICH I BE FATED TO LEAD INTO ASGARD ON THE EVE OF ITS DESTRUCTION, CLAIMING THE SLAIN FOR MY OWN. MY SPIRITS LIFTED AT THE THOUGHT--BUT 'TWAS NOT TO BE, THE RAGNAROK WAS A *FALSE* ONE, BROUGHT ABOUT BY THY TRICKERY.** THUS, E'EN MINE ORDAINED MISSION WAS DENIED ME.

I WEPT...AND PLOTTED MY REVENGE. WHILE THOU WERT OCCUPIED ELSEWHERE, I SEIZED VALHALLA, THY PRIZED DOMAIN, REMAKING IT AS NIFFLEHEIM, THAT ITS SOULS SWORE ALLEGIANCE ONLY TO ME. I SLEW YOUR VALKYRIES THAT YOU WOULD KNOW ANGUISH AND LOSS SUCH AS I HAVE SUFFERED. 'TWAS ALL FUTILE, NOTHING WAS GAINED. I SEE THAT NOW.

HELA, NOT E'EN ODIN CHOSE TO BE ODIN. WHAT IS....IS. WE BE ALL CREATURES OF NECESSITY. AND NOT ALL THY TEARS MAY CHANGE THAT.

WOULD THAT I COULD OFFER THEE *HOPE,* BUT I CANST NOT.

HOPE DOTH BLOSSOM IN THE PRESENCE OF LIFE...AND THOU ART THE QUEEN OF DEATH.

BUT I MAY GRANT THEE ENLIGHTENMENT, OPEN THY MIND....LET MY WISDOM FLOW INTO THEE...

...AND THOU WILL UNDERSTAND THE WAY OF THE WORLD.

THERE SHALL BE NO PUNISHMENT FOR THEE. THOU HAST ONLY THE PITY OF ODIN. I CARE FOR THEE...

...AS DO I ALL MY CHILDREN.